HISTORY OF GOLF

KENNY ABDO

Fly!
An Imprint of Abdo Zoom
abdobooks.com

abdobooks.com

Published by Abdo Zoom, a division of ABDO, P.O. Box 398166, Minneapolis, Minnesota 55439. Fly!™ is a trademark and logo of Abdo Zoom.

Printed in the United States of America, North Mankato, Minnesota.
052019
092019

THIS BOOK CONTAINS RECYCLED MATERIALS

Photo Credits: Alamy, AP Images, Granger Collection, Icon Sportswire, iStock, Shutterstock
Production Contributors: Kenny Abdo, Jennie Forsberg, Grace Hansen
Design Contributors: Dorothy Toth, Neil Klinepier

Library of Congress Control Number: 2018963565

Publisher's Cataloging-in-Publication Data

Names: Abdo, Kenny, author.
Title: History of golf / by Kenny Abdo.
Description: Minneapolis, Minnesota : Abdo Zoom, 2020 | Series: History of sports | Includes online resources and index.
Identifiers: ISBN 9781532127403 (lib. bdg.) | ISBN 9781532128387 (ebook) | ISBN 9781532128875 (Read-to-me ebook)
Subjects: LCSH: Golf--History--Juvenile literature. | Golf--Juvenile literature. | Sports--History--Juvenile literature.
Classification: DDC 796.35209--dc23

TABLE OF CONTENTS

GOLF

Teeing off in the 1400's, golf has withstood the test of time and has become a major sport throughout the world!

Golf is played on a course that usually has 18 holes. Players use a variety of **clubs** to get their golf balls into each hole in as few **strokes** as possible.

WARM UP

Modern day golf is traced back to Scotland in the mid-1400s. The sport was banned by the Scottish government because they thought it interfered with military training.

The first golf balls were made of feathers wrapped in leather. Wood balls were in use by the mid-1800s. Instead of **tees**, golfers would hit the ball from a mound of sand.

There are four major golf tournaments. They are the Masters, the US Open, the Open **Championship**, and the PGA Championship. Golfers from around the world play to prove who the best really is.

ANNUAL
CHAMPIONSHIP
OF THE
PROFESSIONAL
GOLFERS
ASSOCIATION
OF
AMERICA
RODMAN WANAMAKER
TROPHY

The first PGA **Championship** was played in 1916. Jim Barnes walked away with $500 and a diamond-studded gold medal. The first Women's PGA Championship was played in 1955. Beverly Hanson **clinched** the **title** and earned $1,200.

TITLEHOLDERS
CHAMPION

BIG SHOW

Park Sung-hyun was named the best golfer by the Women's World Golf Rankings in 2017. She won the Women's PGA **Championship** in 2018.

Hana
Financial Group
nk
work

USA

Brooks Koepka is a rising star in the world of professional golf. Koepka is one of only five players in the history of golf to win the US Open and PGA **Championship** in the same year!

USGA

Tiger Woods has been called the greatest golfer to ever walk the **links**. He hit his first **hole-in-one** when he was just eight years old! Woods has won more than 80 PGA events, including the 2019 Masters!

GLOSSARY

championship – a game held to find a first-place winner.

clinch – to confirm a win.

club – a slender shaft with a wood or iron head that is used for hitting the golf ball. They come in different sizes to hit the ball different distances.

hole-in-one – a shot in golf that enters the hole from the tee with no other shots in between.

links – another term for a golf course.

stroke – hitting or attempting to hit the golf ball as one point.

tee – a small wooden peg where the golf ball is set to be hit.

tee off – to begin a round or a single hole of golf.

title – a first-place position in a contest.

ONLINE RESOURCES

Booklinks
NONFICTION NETWORK
FREE! ONLINE NONFICTION RESOURCES

To learn more about golf, please visit abdobooklinks.com or scan this QR code. These links are routinely monitored and updated to provide the most current information available.

INDEX